BABY DAZE

POEMS ABOUT EARLY MOTHERHOOD

SARAH DAVIS

The Book Guild Ltd

First published in Great Britain in 2018 by
The Book Guild Ltd
9 Priory Business Park
Wistow Road, Kibworth
Leicestershire, LE8 0RX
Freephone: 0800 999 2982
www.bookguild.co.uk
Email: info@bookguild.co.uk
Twitter: @bookguild

Typeset in Minion Pro

Printed and bound in Great Britain by 4edge Limited

ISBN 978 1912362 134

British Library Cataloguing in Publication Data.
A catalogue record for this book is available from the British Library.

Printed on FSC accredited paper

To my husband John Davis thank you for your love and support over the last twenty-one years. Thank you for the many happy times we've had together just the two of us and as a family. Our life has followed a very different path to how we envisaged it but as a couple we've met the challenges that life has thrown at us along the way and I love you.

To Matthew our long waited for and very precious son (now aged five) – without your inspiration these poems would never have been written – I love you very much and I'm so lucky to be your mummy.

CONTENTS

GETTING TO KNOW YOU

The scan and seeing the beating of your tiny little heart,
Knowing that it's really only just the very start.

Growing ever bigger as you struggle to find room.
Feeling kicks and hiccups as you move inside the womb.

Hearing your first cries just as you come into the world
Beginning your life's journey – soon to be unfurled.

The gripping of my finger with your tiny little hand
The feelings and emotions only parents understand.

WAITING

Rows and rows of baby clothes are waiting in the drawer
My bag is packed and ready – it's waiting by the door.
The question is my patience – how will I survive?
All these days of waiting till you're ready to arrive?

Boy or girl, whichever – doesn't matter either way.
What I know already is I love you more each day
I've been reading leaflets and baby books galore!
Nothing will prepare me though for what I have in
store!

The time that I've spent waiting has put me to the test
Waiting for the moment that they lay you on my chest.
When I get to hold you when you're only seconds old
And family life together can start to unfold.

PREMATURE

Four weeks early – I can't believe
I didn't get on maternity leave.
Had no time to fret or worry
You were clearly in a hurry!

Went to work in the usual way
At first a normal, average day.
I really didn't suspect a thing
No idea what that day would bring!

I had a few pains and rang to say
I thought you might be on your way.
Within four hours you were there!
Just enough time for gas and air!

The birth day of my precious boy
Brought with it so much love and joy!
I'm glad I didn't have to wait
Patiently for your due date.

BIRTH

One more push might do it
I give it my all and you're here.
"Is baby OK?
It's a boy!
I have a son!
I'm a mum!"
They whisk you away for checks
A few puffs of oxygen – you're fine!
As they put you on me skin to skin
My beaming smile says it all.

OUR LITTLE MIRACLE

One born every minute
That's as maybe – but not to us
Our precious first born.
Transfixed by your every sound and move
Watching your chest rise and fall
Our little miracle.

One born every minute
That's as maybe – but not to us
In those first minutes
Lost in the moment our world stood still
You've changed our lives forever
Our little miracle.

One born every minute
That's as maybe – but not to us
Birth – a natural thing
Every day, all over the world
But to us you'll always be
Our little miracle.

YOU'RE HERE

We've waited for so many years
Through all the heartache and the tears.

Words can't describe my beaming smile
You've made the journey all worthwhile.

Feelings so strong within my heart
The rest of my life can finally start.

Huge emotion fills my chest
As they put you to my breast.

My baby you have no idea
How much it means to hold you here.

I hope through time you'll get to see
Just how much you mean to me.

POST NATAL

When you've just been through labour
There's nothing left to see!
Your pride was left at the front door
Along with dignity!

You have a new priority
Your newborn baby's care
No chance to think about yourself
You have no time to spare!

Although the learning curve is steep
From when they cut the cord.
Becoming a new parent is
A really great reward!

ON THE WARD

The women all around you
Understand what you've been through.
You're all learning together
The things you have to do.

You talk to complete strangers
Like they're friends you've known for years.
As new mums you are sharing
Similar joys and fears.

With people who relate to
The position that you're in
If you are very lucky
Lasting friendships can begin.

DISCHARGED / HOMECOMING

We've spent some time in hospital,
Been caring for your needs
Learning everything we can
About nappies, wind and feeds.

They're letting you come home with us
And although we're very proud
As we're still such novices
Should that really be allowed?

We've dressed you up to shield you
From the coolness of the night
And checked with all the midwives
That everything's alright.

We've put you very gently
In the car seat with such care
Avoiding every bump and pot hole
Soon we will be there.

We've carried you in carefully
And quietly closed the door
Thinking of the family fun
That we will have in store.

REGISTERING YOUR BIRTH

We've had many conversations
About what would be your name.
We decided years ago
And it's always stayed the same.

Today we're off to the Town Hall
To record it officially.
It will be there in black and white
For everyone to see.

You'll have a special certificate
With our family details.
We'll sort out all the paperwork
And all that it entails.

A copy will be taken
And future family
Will be able to refer to it
And see their ancestry.

NIGHT NOISES

It's not just your cries for feeding
That cause me to awake.
It's all the other night time noises
That you always make!

Sniffles and snuffles
Fidgets and shuffles
Grunts and groans
Gasps and moans
Wheezing and croaking
Coughing and choking
Cries and simpers
Coos and whimpers

While you just lie there sleeping
(Though it may be my mistake)
It seems it's your intention
To keep Mummy wide awake!!

HEALTH VISITORS

As mother to a newborn
We are keen to do what's right
To ensure that baby's safe
Throughout every day and night.

Though guidelines should be followed
So we don't make big mistakes
We develop our own instincts
And we soon learn what it takes.

The most helpful thing I learned,
That's stood me in good stead,
Was early on at clinic
When the health visitor said:

"Take on board all our advice
And all that we suggest
Then make your own decisions
And do what you think is best!"

OUR WASHING MACHINE

It seems our trusty washing machine's
Become our greatest friend.
The trail of dirty clothes you leave
Never seems to end!

The sound of the spin cycle
Signals that the washing's done
But before I get to hang it out
A new pile has begun!

GRANDPARENTS

"Hello, darling! Grandma's here!"
She walks in grinning from ear to ear.
Grandad follows in close pursuit
Bearing groceries, nappies and fruit.
It's been three days since they were here
Their rapturous cries suggest a year!
It's not just babysitting tots
They do our laundry and wash our pots.
So when you're sleeping we can too
And spend more quality time with you
And what's more they have the grace
To know when what we want is space
They let us know how much they care
And if we want advice it's there
I hope they know we hold them dear
It means so much to have them near.

MUMS AND BABIES GROUP

My local mums and babies group
Helps to keep me sane
With adult conversation
To stimulate my brain.

When I am feeling anxious
It helps to get me through
To hear that all the other mums
Have fears and worries too.

We talk about our babies
And get stuff off our chest
And reassure each other
We can only do our best.

We have a laugh and giggle
About the week we've had
Sharing our experience
The good things and the bad.

By the time our tea is finished
And we've put the world to rights
We're re-energised to face
Another week of sleepless nights.

A HUMAN MILK MACHINE

I'm a human milk machine
Got no time to cook or clean!
Not much time between the feeds
To get to see to Mummy's needs!
Laughable the mere suggestion
Of meals without indigestion!
Whatever happened to personal care?
Its three days since I washed my hair!
Dad will be home in an hour
I might get chance to have a shower!
We know who is in charge round here
Someone makes that very clear!
With his daily bath to keep him clean
And 'feed on demand' dictating routine.

COMMUNICATION

Every baby's different
No one rule fits them all
It isn't very easy
Looking after one so small!

The tears of a newborn baby
Test the patience of a saint!
Leaving parents feeling
Overtired and often faint.

If only they could tell us
The cause of their loud cry
We would be much more able
To help or pacify.

But we learn to read their signals
And interpret their small cues
And in turn develop strategies
That we begin to use.

And in return they give us
That tiny baby smile
Telling us we're doing well
And making it worthwhile!

BABY DAZE

I'm walking round in a daze
'Baby Brain' – a well-coined phrase!
I haven't come back down to earth
Since the day that I gave birth!

Countless things I've left undone
Since I've had my little one.
Without my handy 'To do' list
Goodness knows what I'd have missed!

I've been assured "it's baby brain"
And not that I have gone insane.
I'm hoping soon the tide will turn
And my 'pre-baby' brain return.

FIRST TRIP ALONE /
NIPPING TO THE POST BOX

I'm just nipping out.
If he needs me please shout.
He's just been fed
And put to bed.
You know where things are.
I'm taking the car.
I'd better make tracks
I'll be five minutes max!
I'll get on my way
If you're sure you're OK?
I know – you're his dad!!
But I still feel bad!!
OK!! I'm going!!!

BEING MUM

She cares for me
Looking after my needs – feeding, clothing and changing
me

She teaches me
Introducing me to the world and all its opportunities

She entertains me
Taking me for walks, playing and singing to me

She loves me
Providing me with comfort and cuddles – soothing my
cries

And in return?

I gaze back at her – with my toothless grin
And love in my eyes.

NIGHT FEEDS

Woken abruptly in the night
In the middle of a dream
By your baby letting out
A very hungry scream!

No time to get up slowly
The amount of noise he makes
You're leaping quickly out of bed
Before the whole house wakes!

The inevitable happens
Before feeding can begin
His nappy needs a change
Amid the yelling and the din!

He's not heard of patience
And does not want to wait
The intensity increases
And the cries just escalate!

When the feeding time is done
You get back to bed fast
And get the sleep you can
Because you know the peace won't last!

A MUM'S LAMENT

Oh whatever can I do?
Up to my eyes in nappies and poo!
Baby has been up all night!
Will I ever get it right?

Tried to sing a lullaby
My Auntie Jean says "Let him cry!"
Not the same from Auntie Jo
Who'd pick him up and not let go!

It isn't that I mind advice
Consistency would just be nice!
Peace at last – there is a lull
Life with a newborn's never dull!

NAPPY DAYS

Oh my goodness he's not happy
He has got a filthy nappy!
He just let out such a trump
The explosion made me jump!
Catapulted him off my knee
Hardly dared to look and see!
It's on his back and legs as well
I can't describe the awful smell!
I had better make it snappy
His feet are getting in the nappy!
I'm worried about his poorly tum
Don't want to seem a fussy mum!
But it has given me a fright
I want to check that he's alright.
Doctor said that this much poo
Is common – "It's what babies do!"

ROLY POLIES

We can't change your nappy
When you're rolling round and round.
We weren't anticipating
This new game that you've found.

When you first did roly polies
You'd hear us say, "Well done!"
But in the middle of a change
For us it's not much fun!

You seem to think its funny
Why aren't we laughing too?
But we can't have roly polies
With a nappy full of poo!

You're flipping your legs over
And your bottom's in the air
Nappy change a two-man job
We have no hands to spare!

Then when the struggle's over
You look up with a grin
As if to say "We're done now!"
Let the wriggling begin!

GOING OUT

Been up all night!
I look a fright!
My hair and nerves on end!

We're running late!
A shower can wait!
I'm only meeting a friend.

Pram's in boot
I'd better scoot
Where have I put my keys?

I know well
That awful smell!
No! Not a nappy – please!!!!

Of times he picks
He always sticks
To when we're going out

But my baby boy
Is my pride and joy
Who I wouldn't be without!

PUBLIC APPEARANCE

Getting you anywhere on time
Is always a bit of a pantomime!

We can't even get to the end of our street
Without being stopped by the neighbours we meet!
They look in the pram and gasp "How you've grown!"
You're a mini celebrity all on your own!

When we were out at the shop last week
A stranger came over to take a peek.
She commented on your tiny, wee socks
And gave you a coin for your money box!

A new experience this for me
It's like being out with royalty!
Make the most of it while you can
Keep grinning back at them my little man!

PUBLIC CONVERSATIONS

Before becoming parents
We had made a vow
Not to have the conversations
That we're doing now!

We'd heard lots of other people
While lunching in the pub
Saying things to babies
That put us off our grub!

But when you are so busy
You may forget just how it felt
To hear talk of smelly bottoms
While enjoying tuna melt!

We do try to be thoughtful
And keep our voices low
So those around don't hear things
That they do not want to know!

BABY GYM

No need to pay for a gym fee
My fitness programme is for free
Up and down the stairs all day
Crouching on the mat to play
Holding baby above my head
Lifting him in and out of bed
Losing fat with every feed
What more workout do I need?

NIGHT WATCH

Watching you lying in your bed,
Snuggled up with Little Ted,
Listening to my lullabies,
Little smiles, coos and cries.
Through half closed lids you smile and peep
While I rock you off to sleep.
My baby boy you're growing fast
Sleeping through the night at last!

PHONE CALL TO A FRIEND

"Hi! Yes I can chat!
How about that?
He's enjoying his feeding time
So it won't be the usual pantomime!
Oooh – Did she really?
That'll cost her dearly!
Sorry – I've just heard him cry
He might settle – it's worth a try.
It's alright now – he's playing.
Now what were you saying?
Oh! Hang on a minute!
He's got his hands in it!!
I'll ring you later!"

BATH TIME FOR BOYS

Mummy bought Daddy an apron
To save him from getting wet
Not just from the bath water
But from your inbuilt directional jet!

BABY BATH

You really love your bath time
Smiling, having fun
Kicking your little legs about
And splashing everyone!

We love to hear your giggles
As the bubbles fly about
But at the end its always
Much more tough to get you out.

Then with the towel we dry you
From your head down to your toes
Eyes and mouth just peeking out
With your tiny button nose.

Then it's time for snuggles
In your little babygro
And cosy in your basket
Off to sleepy land you go.

BALANCING ACT

Life's an endless cycle
Of nappies, chores and feeds!
It really is a full time job
Caring for your needs!

I sometimes find I grimace
When I see the laundry pile!
But seeing that you're happy
Makes each busy day worthwhile!

Because between the many tasks
And work that's to be done.
We always seem to find the time
To have a lot of fun!

We watch you laugh and giggle
As we sing you nursery rhymes
Playing with your many toys
Enjoying happy times!

LEARNING

Watching the world around you
Learning more each day
Responding to sounds and voices
Finding new ways to play.

Responding to colourful patterns
And different textures too
By reaching out and grabbing
Finding out what you can do.

It's fun to watch you learning
As you discover each new place.
Little things that cause a smile
To spread across your face.

CAMERA SHY

What's that you're pointing at me?
I don't like it very much!
It isn't even something
That I'm allowed to touch!

It stops me seeing you Mummy!
Hides your face from view!
When I am busy smiling
Right back up at you!

You might be disappointed
Every time you bring it out.
At first I look quite puzzled
And then begin to pout.

My smiles are for you Mummy!
Not meant for all to see!
Just enjoy the moment
And forget posterity!

BABY TALK

Your skills in conversation
Are developing each day
Helping you communicate
In your own special way.

Your face is more expressive
Helping us to read your needs
Giving us new signals
For attention or for feeds.

Your excited coos and squeals
Tell us you're having fun
And you've learnt to laugh and chuckle
Along with everyone.

BREAST FEEDING

I wanted to give my baby
The start they recommend
And now my days of mummy milk
Are coming to an end.

My baby's doing really well
Growing fit and strong
And he'll be on solids
Before too very long.

Soggy breast pads, leaking milk
Will all be in the past
The electric breast pump
Will be put away at last.

Getting my own body back
No longer fantasy
And night time feeding on demand
A fading memory.

SOLID FOODS

Mashed up sweet potato
And pureed carrot paste
Just a little on a spoon
To get used to the taste.

On your clothes and up the wall
You're making such a mess!
Is any in your mouth at all?
It's anybody's guess!

No! The spoon is not designed
To catapult your food!
And when at someone else's house
It is considered rude.

But you are showing interest
And that is good to know
You're obviously having fun
And learning as you go!

FAMILY MEALS OUT

Taking baby out when weaning
Can be an ordeal
Especially if he's having
Pureed carrot for his meal!

Try dressing him in orange
It's a very useful tip
Instead of lots of changing
It helps conceal each drip!

You've no time for fashion
Or designer wear
You have barely had the time
To shower and wash your hair!

Forget what suits your colouring
As by the end of the night
Your jumper will be orange
Though it started out as white!

TIME TOGETHER

Tiny fingers, tiny toes
Little vests and babygros.
Changing, feeding, playing too
Countless days just me and you.
Growing closer day by day
The world outside just fades away.
Making the most with my little one
Maternity leave will soon be done.

MEMORIES

I'm sure that you have no idea
The pleasure that it brings
To watch you changing every day
Discovering new things.

We're storing up these memories
As you are growing fast
And we know that your baby days
Are quickly flying past.

We'll look back on these precious times
Remembering with joy
The very special moments
Spent with our baby boy.

THE FUTURE

I'm sure that in the future
We'll have many conversations
When you will tell us all about
Your plans and aspirations.

I hope that you will use
The many things that you've been taught
And we will be right there
If you want guidance or support.

You know we'll always love you
Whichever path you choose
Whichever of your skills and talents
You decide to use.

When it comes right down to it
What I want most for you
Is independence, health and happiness
And to have your dreams come true.

ACKNOWLEDGEMENTS

My family – thank you for all you have done for me.

Cathie Kelly, for your much-valued friendship over the past thirty-five years – who knew we'd still be friends all these years after school? Thank you for your constructive comments about these poems. I knew I could rely on you to be both honest and supportive.

Ros and Anne, my colleagues, whose Saturday afternoon shift at Horsforth Library got disrupted by me going into early and fairly fast labour!

Moyra and Peter, who had the unexpected task of driving me to hospital that afternoon with my contractions just a few minutes apart – I couldn't ask for better in-laws than you two – thank you for everything you do for us all!

The staff at Seacroft Hospital and those at LGI in neo-natal and transitional care.

Sue Bordley for keeping me going in my final year at college and being my friend ever since.

My more recent 'mum' friends – the people I turn to in the crazy world of parenthood and whose support, encouragement and advice I value. Too many to name you all individually but you know who you are Treetops Mums and school mums – thank you. Thank you in particular to Claire Dawson, Vicky Blake, Juliana Rosero Calad and Rebecca Whittington – not just for your friendship but also for your encouragement with this book.

Richard O'Donnell (who shares my love of writing creatively) thank you for being a great head teacher to work for over many years, for your interesting advice and perspectives and for sharing your enthusiastic opinions about my writing and encouraging me with this book.

Finally thank you again to John and Matthew – for everything!